DROLLERIES

ALSO BY CASSIDY McFADZEAN

Hacker Packer

DROLLERIES

Cassidy McFadzean

McClelland and Stewart

Library and Archives Canada Cataloguing in Publication

McFadzean, Cassidy, author
Drolleries / Cassidy McFadzean.

Poems.
Issued in print and electronic formats.
ISBN 978-0-7710-7317-5 (softcover). – ISBN 978-0-7710-7318-2 (EPUB)

I. Title.

PS8625.F35D76 2019   C811'.6   C2018-903243-X
                                             C2018-903244-8

Published simultaneously in the United States of America by
McClelland & Stewart, a division of Penguin Random House Canada
Limited, a Penguin Random House Company.

Typeset in Janson by M&S, Toronto
Printed and bound in Canada

McClelland & Stewart,
a division of Penguin Random House Canada Limited,
a Penguin Random House Company
www.penguinrandomhouse.ca

I   2   3   4   5   23   22   21   20   19

Penguin
Random House
McCLELLAND & STEWART

to Nathan

CONTENTS

Glasses, glasses is the only drinking: and for thy walls, a pretty slight drollery, or the story of the Prodigal, or the German hunting in water-work, is worth a thousand of these bed-hangings and these fly-bitten tapestries.

Shakespeare
Henry IV, Part 2

DROLLERIES

NYMPH

Forest pine needles formed a false floor
that broke away below me, earth

loosening around the roots
of a rotting log's hollow chambers.

I fell ass-first in the dappled brook,
grasping moss-covered rocks,

and scrambled uphill as twigs gashed
my legs, leaving two thin thistle kisses.

To stop myself from slipping
into a nearby fox den, I clasped

half a sheep skull – purple collagen
hardened to ridged teeth – and skimmed

my hand against a lichen-flecked trunk,
a smooth rail that pulled me upright.

I held tightly to snapping branches
as maggots danced, then vanished.

Suspended between certain dirt
and a glossy cobweb caught at head height,

the tree's outstretched hand took hold
of my ring and wedded itself to me.

SATURNALIA

Someone left a sliver in my big toe.
By Cassini's rings, was it you?

I shattered a glass on the counter.
When one ring falls, the rest follow through . . .

Those shards of ice scattered
into invisible meteorites across the floor,

brushed my legs and feet with abrasions.
I was cut by grass bending in a fierce breeze,

and dabbed at the injuries, but my blood dried.
Outside, a field of wheat moved as a single mind,

lowering its blades to peasants' scythes.
Like Levin's slow-mowed sickle,

I hunger for such synchrony.
I've found the feeling of sisterhood rarely.

Was it only in the company of men?
When we're each of us in our bleeding,

and might speak to matters of the abdomen,
then it's moonlets and stars that ground me.

In morning, my wool-bound feet can't walk
for limping over craters.

My kitchen's crystals gleam at me,
gag gifts winking in their twinning.

MERCURY

I saw a stream of silver
leave your mouth, he said,

teasing the wisp of mercury,
a lizard's tail, out of me.

When Hermes hung retrograde,
we wandered aisles carrying

mandrake, nightshade, canned
half-moon hearts of palm.

It was the eve of another news
anchor's son's fentanyl death.

Climbing a mountain with no peak,
we wanted to numb ourselves

for the fun of it, little dogs
gnawing at scraps of meat.

Was that when you entered?
Turning away invites you in,

your hand between my thighs,
feeling for an opening.

JANUS

The shower curtain's spots
of black mould were constellations
in the shape of larkspur,

cultivars the tapestries marked noxious.
That cold morning I swallowed
mouthfuls of spores as droplets struck,

clusters of fungi staining my lungs.
We were children again,
whispering under glow-in-the-dark stars

that dimmed as we slept.
One of us faced the bookcase;
the other faced the wall.

ILL OMENS

She woke in the dark,
stricken with a premonition:
my body on a stretcher,

a vision of my impending trip.
My mother's third eye peered
into her crystal ball of night

and found me brain-dead.
Insisting I take a taxi in the city,
not get lost on subways,

nor split my head open, nor fall,
her worry became a cure-all.
Mother, crone, soothsayer,

she listened as my once-halting
speech cleared to a wisp of ink
billowing in the scrying bowl.

I shied from her praise, loath
to see shame rooted within –
not spectre of myself, but twin.

GALLERY OF GEMS

A mouse scratches its way
through my head, clawing deeper

each time I blink my eyes.
Alone in the museum I buy

a gold-leaf laurel necklace, direct
a woman to Ancient Greece.

A wall of geodes appears
as a doorway I enter.

Cavities lined with amethyst,
the sharp edges of my brain.

When the subway swerves
around the junction, it captures

the city as a closing aperture
in an iPhone's reflection.

A woman teaches her son to say
Garbage, repeat after me. I turn away,

I can't eat. I have a weakness
in me that attracts others

who are weak. Ice crystallizes
on the window, tiny trees.

POMPEII

Through the stereoscope's 3-D,
I see myself preserved in ash
in a glass cage. I return to Pompeii

in the museum alone, a model
of city walls, Mount Vesuvius looming.
You said we narrowly missed

a landslide of hurt, like villagers
who, fleeing the shooting pumice,
somehow made it to safety.

The dog chained outside the brothel
wasn't so lucky. We worshipped
Bacchus on the volcano's fertile

land. Drank Thanksgiving night
as tremors rattled underground.
Years ago, you told me to feed

the monster inside, and I did.
My cellphone became a bulla
I clasped to my chest waiting

for you to return my text,
and tell me if we'd flee or burn.
Screens display our final moments:

the dormouse fattened for feasting,
figs in a bowl blackened to pits.
Here is a charred loaf of bread.

Here is a middle-aged man proud
of his accomplishments. Mars's
affair with already-married Venus

teaches us that love prevails.
My mother's premonition
I'd end up brain-dead I took

as an omen to stop using my head.
Our eruption was Plinian, flash heat
contracting our muscles to climax.

MOOD

Witch hazel in my pussy.
Rose water on the brain.
Let's not go down memory lane,
but memory locker, feelings stored away.

I keep my garbage in the freezer
just like this city taught me.
I know it's love, when during sex,
my new lover wipes my ass for me.

Zip up your feelings, Will advised
looking over the Brooklyn Bridge.
I watch a man zip his pet rat
into his jacket on the subway.

Have I ruined another group chat?
Have I repressed a painful memory?
I say goodbye with vocal fry
so I can feel it in my body.

TEN OF SWORDS

This island's where the lonely go
on holiday weekends away from home.
I came here to think things through . . .

Like, if my father figures stop trying
to fuck me, will I still have daddy issues?
At the petting zoo a penned-in pig

pressed his head against the grate,
mewling till my fingers graze him.
Poetry means never being sated.

For the first time, when the male gaze
follows my miniskirt down the street
I reciprocate. Your hand on my leg

shows me the place you dream –
we can meet there in our sleep.
Fruit flies followed us from bar

to bar, hovering above our bodies.
Parasites: medieval haloes of desire.
I heard a fly buzz when I read

my poems at Tony Roma's. In bed
I told my husband, "I'm your wife."
He answered back, "A witch."

ASPECT OF SATURN

Encircled by words,
as Huygens at 27, struck **by**
Saturn's curious "extensions," **a**
ring, solid, surrounding the planet.
His engravings are delicate, **thin,**
and touch Saturn like eyelids held
flat against an iris urn. Maria Clara's
blue renditions were **nowhere**
touching the crude. Her drawings
were amalgamations, **inclined**
to aesthetics, captured

the deliberately obtuse, **the**

ecliptic.

IN THE FOREST

Somewhere's a frond,
a leaf under a canopy
of deciduous trees in the colonies,

blades jackknifed under jack pines,
in places settlers now occupy.
Ferns shied away from our fingers' touch,

from humans and our taxonomy.
Some we called *Mimosa pudica*,
the shrinking, sensitive plant,

one that furls its bashful leaves
then uncurls in ten to fifteen minutes,
once the unpleasantness proceeds.

Its shyness is only momentary,
the passing glimpse of a lunar eclipse,
a vision that disturbs, then languishes.

Sometimes grazing the fern with fingers
fans its lapsing. Sometimes it closes
against the heat of a forest in flames.

When policemen entered the woods,
did you stop running to record
the fern's peaceful curl?

Will you, too, write poems about trees
when the woods are full of police?

DEATH MARCH SESTINA

From Berlin to Krakow we rode the train,
passing a forest where snow clung to trees,
a layer of white over chimney dust,
cottages growing from charred ground.
As saplings reached for sunlight,
I blocked the glare with my hands.

Seventy years earlier, starving men handled
a rusted tin can's lid thrown from a train.
They held the scrap of metal lightly,
grated the tool against the bark of trees.
Cut with a dozen jagged holes, it ground
the dried bark into a fine, grey dust.

They mixed water with collected dust,
creating a thick paste in their hands.
The taste was like muddied groundwater.
Can the human body, with time, train
itself to survive, even off the stuff of trees?
The uniformed captors lit

the path in flickering orange light.
Flames spread like cosmic dust
as men found discarded canisters under trees,
openings sliced into metal lids, handed
over and tossed in a pile like bodies from trains.
How will mothers explain these grounds

to their children? The models of grounds
were displayed in museum light,
miniature tracks leading tiny trains,
where writhing faces became a pile of dust.
Behind us, was it one of those hands
that carved a branch of the Goethe tree?

It wasn't hard to see the emaciated bodies as trees
feeding on themselves, scattered over ground.
The branches were reaching hands
in a sky somehow still filled with light.
The forest's monolith became dust
as we moved away in the passenger train.

Our hands gripped the steel of the train
as bodies underground breathed dust,
trees disappearing in the morning light.

The shiny parts a magpie has gathered to build its nest

Too much batter poured into a muffin tin's segments

More strung-out succulent than tightly wound rosette

The plastic tote trays of the Domesday seed vault, flooded

VENUS OF MADRID

O pilaster with tendrils and birds,
I want the lightness of your flowers
carved in stone to inscribe itself in me,

Ara Pacis: happiness, abundance, peace.
Am I your wingless Cupid, a metal
torch in each dumb servant hand,

or twin-figured Eros and Aphrodite?
We know the muse of dance is headless,
the raving of maenads unrestrained.

In transparent dresses, women abandon
their bodies to music like I never could,
all my days spent behind a sheet of glass.

I'm the ochre fixed to the rounded snout
of the stone horse. Years from now you'll
find me here, hard thing hinting at light.

LEAVING THE ATOCHA STATION

I can't stay here anymore
in my body, where it's difficult

not to ideate the oncoming train.
I ask you how *Anna Karenina* ends

and you tell me, closing the book
and stepping out into the world.

In our rented bachelor suite
a toilet gleams behind a glass partition.

No door handles in the Airbnb
but a series of locks

and one set of keys. I take off
my wedding ring when I feel

a rat scratching in the walls,
metal sticking in noonday heat.

HOLY WOUNDS

Christ's wound is the open mouth
of the grinning face emoji, lips
dripping Smucker's red raspberry jam.

In the tale of Nastagio degli Onesti,
marriage meant a knight hunting
the ungrateful woman, hounds

nipping her thighs until he flung
her heart to their waiting teeth.
The punishment repeated each Friday.

Like Saint Michael slaying Lucifer
ad nauseum, the action becomes
a monster itself, a kaleidoscope

gone awry, early '90s Magic Eye.
Aventurine lends the adoration
of shepherds a glittering backdrop

as old ladies' swollen feet press
against leather sandals on Spanish
streets, thyroids like pelicans' gullets

spitting phlegm over concrete.
One night, I dreamed my skin peeled
away, shedding a sunburnt chrysalis

on our bedding, never fully drying
in this humidity. The peppery scent
of the botanical gardens mixed

with the tree-of-heaven's semen
stink, and followed us to the subway
like piss-dripping bags of garbage.

THE WAY

If the forest opened itself to me,
how deeply would I follow it inside?
Or if you dropped pebbles to follow,
would I allow you to invite me in,
to enter your home, to use the toilet,
let me be enwrapped in a stranger's arms?
Nearly two minutes in, I remembered

I'd forgotten about rape, mislaid
the notion of fear, prompted by the man
clad in Lycra shorts jogging toward me,
body sweat a glaze. His gaze surveyed me.
Distant beasts brayed to the rhythm of his
ample breathing. I found my SMS
wouldn't send. So if I fell surrounded

by trees and Nature – so be it – released
of physical being I felt it all: fear, lust,
a body weighed down with plastic beads,
whose shadow flitted past hickory.
The matter was taken from me, a child's,
and seized. I embraced my slumping to see
where the unfamiliar posture would lead.

A pale cicada curled at my feet.
I imagined the life I still wanted:
my cursor blinking on a dizzied screen.
In a world that's mainly insects, did I move
in it too heavily? I fished a fly
from a cobweb and it flew into me,
squandered freedom colliding with atoms

as we all do. In the forest's gentle clearing,
a dog-walker found me wandering
and helped me find the way. We looked
over the graveyard and each blotch she read
on my face she saw as brush strokes – not wings.
I turned back at the cemetery's gate,
and lost myself in the forest again.

TO FIND A GHOST FOREST

Search first for traces of charcoal
blackening the pathway, trees felled
for fuel where livestock once grazed.
Unearth clues obscured in old maps
and estate records, spectres of shadow
woods archived in the king's Domesday.
The phantoms cling to honeysuckle,
holly, common cow-wheat, haunting
hacked-off limbs of coppiced trees.
Bluebells mark woodland turned
to pasture, a ring of hanging heads
announcing the forest's neat graves.

GHOSTING

If I wear enough concealer
will I disappear completely,

blend in with the mirrors,
assume a new personality?

I saw a real-life mummy
and put its JPEG on my laptop screen.

Now my computer's haunted,
a MacBook-of-the-dead

whose powers and spells
I'll harness to guide me.

Give me the strength, Lindow Man,
for ghosting this life:

so tired am I of never picking
the burned piece of cake

in the druid's bannock ritual,
of missing the mistletoe,

of each night's party ending
with "Dancing on My Own."

CLINTING IN THE WOODS

I found a pair of velvet-covered antlers.
Three fingers reached from an open palm
still throbbing with platelet's hot breath,

grave markings perched on snow.
I clasped the shed horns, abandoned
by some migrating buck, triple brow tine

doubtless cast from a fervent rut, and slid
the pulsing things into my rucksack,
clanging against my canteen and matches.

A slit was cut in their toes, the split-hoofed
ungulates, seams cleaving in thorny keratin
like threads sewn in wool. In my embroidered

tabi boots, I returned to my winter cabin,
sinking into the crust of my morning steps.
The antlers battered my flesh a bluish hue,

my tender skin stinging when I undressed,
bathwater steaming as my fire crackled
and spat. I sighed and relaxed, conjuring

what I'd once read of the artifact's medicinal
qualities, and examined it under cobalt flame.
Finding the antlers adequate specimens,

I pressed my lips against one thick branch,
tongued the velvet sheathing, and chewed.
I swallowed the fibre as I entered my water,

and within moments, felt tufts of fine hair
as pedicles grew. I was fated, bone collector,
to wander under this same weird moon.

SAGA

Allow me to sing you
the song of my people,
says the common snipe
from Hallgrímskirkja's steeple.

The arctic blue fox
has skin for days.
We removed his sleek fur
with a sharpened blade.

From crown to chandelier
the reindeer's reign passed.
We sucked antler's marrow
and poured a bronze cast.

So many men gathered
in the circle's three rows.
A Britney song was on.
Farmers came to blows.

THE NECROPANTS

The pair of skin slacks was well hung,
in want of a sorcerer to wear them.
Like pantyhose of moulded silicon,
two legs stood behind glass – but
the fabric was epidermis, covered

in hosiery runs of hair that ran
their length, the skin still malleable,
loosened from the flesh and sewn.
Widely rumoured, rarely known,
we gaped before the Necropants.

Though stitching a pair is difficult
even for gifted magicians,
many cunning folk have heard
of the tool to make gold grow,
the nábrók of ancient grimoires.

We know the sorcerer who wishes
to wear this eerie disguise must first
make a pact with a living man's lower
limbs and lap. But what depraved
mind would sanction any old wizard

to dig up his corpse? He must flay it,
careful not to make holes or scratches,
keeping trousers intact from feet
to waistband, allowing another
to prance forth wearing his legs.

What soul could rest knowing
another wore his skin? And worse,
the sorcerer's work was not yet
finished. He must steal a coin
from a poor widow at Christmas,

or Easter, or Whitsun, and slip it –
dare I say – into the empty scrotum.
The magic is such that the Necropants
will draw coins from living souls,
and his crotch will never be empty

when he scratches it. One catch
lets us stomach this perversion:
if the owner fails to gift them before
his mortal passing, his skin will crawl
with lice. He must drop his trousers

before he dies. Once a willing heir
is identified, this new pervert steps
into the right leg before the wizard
exits the left. The task is finished;
his crotch will pay dividends.

FORTUNE

Previews for movies we've already seen comfort
like digging for a stone I know by feel,
engraved with my fortune, hand-picked.

In the night, ice cracks in the AC, waking us.
I turn the dial and hear women yelling
in the street, then a car turning into the alley.

In morning fatigue, my vision settles
on the veins of a woman bagging our groceries
at Bulk Barn. A bulging star, she brandishes

something other-worldly implanted in her.
We want to be stranger than what we are.
I pay what we owe and enter the idling car.

WITCHES' SABBATH

In Goya's reconstructed black room,
me and thirty kindergarteners
watch a dog drown. Call me Asmodea,

the female devil who exposes
the inside of houses like this one,
frescoes stripped from walls.

Domestic taxidermy had us
hovering as I gestured to the life
we were fabricating together,

our every hope lost to the fates,
their scissors cutting what threads of life
I had spooled around my finger.

We transformed into two figures
bludgeoning each other with clubs
in the deaf man's house, X-rays

revealing a grassy meadow we'd lazed
in once. Now I'm a snout whispering
in your ear as you, old man, lean

on your staff. I'm the manola
who, underneath a layer of paint,
appears bare-headed. Veil shed,

I lean on a doorway I might still enter.
I am Judith beheading Holofernes,
the reticent girl transfixed in a chair,

patiently awaiting my initiation
as the cloaked goat's lips part in song.
I'm the monster I knew I was all along.

MIND READER

Nothing was enough: spilled
salt you tossed over your shoulder,
bedstraw I threw in the air.
Spices struck bodies in the bar,

and I asked what I was to you:
two mirrors against each other
forming a chamber of reflections
that wouldn't let you through.

DREAM INTERPRETATION

I dream we veer off a bridge,
the rivers crossed travelling
the Mississippi, the Missouri.
She can't abort the memory
a prairie billboard reads.

Petals fall from the birthday lilies
you bought me, dragonflies
on the windshield hardened to tar.
A quiet murmuring, the woman
on the radio describes a plot

of land lush with greenery.
She took a hoe to her earth
and dug up insulation, raked carpet,
her shovel clanging against tin,
breaking sheets of cloudy glass.

Her fertile land was a dumping
ground, duped by the man
who sold it to her. I dreamed
we dreamed of starting over,
of tilling the earth, seeding it,

cultivating corrugated sheets,
automobile chassis, rebar, green
glass dump with sulphide flower.
Two gravestones fixed in earth,
missing names. They waited for us.

34

CARVE OUT THE EYEHOLE

I kiss that cold space on his cheek,
a corner of light. I'm on top
so it feels like I've got the dick.

Feels good, right?
Waves froth up and rise inside me.
I close one eye and see

the bridge of my nose,
as if looking out of a face.
Rolling hills are *Stone City, Iowa,*

trees an artichoke's leaves.
Texture brings me closer to a tumble,
to absolution. A church

both rubber and angular is what paint is.
Art out of some renaissance brain
but anachronistic, rounded edges

of history and the night
made of dark pigment and light.
He grinds up on me. He smells

like coffee. What is the etymology
of Dilly Bar? We go to a DQ
with a hand-painted sign, order Dickel

Whisky for the stupid rhyme.
I walk home before the thunder
and take pictures of police cruisers,

the park's grass raised
to invisible borders on our bodies.
I pull often to the smooth meat of my brain

grating against carpet fibres.
These twisting fabrics veer within,
silk and static I feel

in my gut, flipped. My knees double
over and fold into self. Love,
I love my body. It helps me see.

ON REMIXING VELÁZQUEZ'S *LAS MENINAS*

Picasso's drawings prefigure Crumb:
prostitute's legs perpetually spread, breasts
perfectly bulbous, a failure of anatomy

in eroticism. A tinny orgy ricochets
from plastic receivers as I approach a couple
sharing one device. Polyamory turns

unsavoury so we part at the gored horse
of Lascaux, the massacre proto-*Guernican*,
grotesque as the kisses of women roaming

the Ramblas with Zara bags. This is me
becoming more and more angular, viewing
Picasso's *Las Meninas* remixes, a portrait

of infant Margarita, heroine of realism
here transformed into triangles, circles, lines.
Every iteration takes Velázquez further

from representation until another angle
emerges – it's the sister who interests him,
she who presents candlestick and flame.

In this act of bestowing, the light is the focus
of each frame, its viewers captivated until
we are all monochrome. Picasso abandons

Velázquez for the dovecote on his balcony:
splayed feathers, pointed beaks, incessant
coos. The Bay of Cannes's distant view.

REAL MADRID

The spring I was only drawing cups and pentacles,
the gold leaf wore off my laurel necklace, metal

plating underneath. Palacio Real's upholstery
matches carpets matching curtains of Gasparini's

room, where the king performed against blue silk walls
the ceremony of getting dressed. Rococo follows

penchant for chinoiserie: plaster foliage against wooden
frames as Atlas bears his globe of constellations,

Spain no comfort for my Taurus sun, made queasy
by swinging pendulums, Aurora gliding across the ceiling.

Posit this: if I were a guest at Maria Cristina's wedding
to the king would I panic and leave? One place

setting out of formation, chair disturbed the slightest bit.
That's me creaking across wooden floors to the exit.

I'm the Real Madrid: holy water resting in a conch,
no food here but for the soul, a woman's matchstick-

patterned blouse a fire hazard to our Airbnb's five
locked doors. In this exquisite stucco room of harpies,

pairs of winged infants bear the insignia of Maria Luisa's
female order. They reprieve Zeus on his eagle,

the throne room's violence, ticking of a distant clock,
Medici lions with their marble ball. Outside the palace

walls, I deal a new spread of swords and wands,
the Spanish Marseilles marking conflict and loss.

STUDY OF A TORSO

When pictures of decapitated journalists
started appearing in my Twitter feed,
their heads lolled in the dirt cartoonishly.
I've been reading the news
so much it's entered me.
In the night I dream I'm raped
in my bed when my husband's away,
the pain in my abdomen so sharp
it wakens me. In a dark room
my iPhone leads me to the law student
who didn't know she'd been attacked
until she viewed it on screen.
She'd said anything to clear his name.
When I drive my husband to Mercy
the third time in as many weeks,
ice obscures the windshield.
I never drive and he makes me brake
so he can get out to clear the ice away,
blood streaking the glass,
globules of flesh smeared on the seat.
A bloody doorknob greets our neighbour,
circular saw still plugged in on the lawn.
I dreamed of it for weeks: his screams,
how much worse it might have been.
I'd asked if I should go back to look
for his fingers, unaware he held them
still attached in hand.
How he'd get me off without them
flashed through my mind even then.
In a room full of brains

I feel the heat of synapses.
I am a flesh marionette, off balance
waiting for the next catastrophe.
A weapon wails from the yard.
I pick my fingers off the floor,
not knowing I had it in me.

PHANTOM LIMB

Before the trash bin, slipping
from my finger as I stick
inside crinkled packaging –
in the water of the lake I swim
like a common nettle stinging
the edges of its band sharpening –
in the cold, my skin constricting
for an instance, the metal loosening –
long since jettisoned, my gold ring
its drop against marble singing –
my indentation lingering, a figment
of freedom and constraint, this wrestling –
a stupid thing, my ruminating –
I still feel it clinging

KUNSTKAMERA

Let us dwell not on how Ruysch's
curiosities fell into brutish hands,
only that Peter the Great transformed
a noble fascination with the human
body into something monstrous,
the mystery of Ruysch's embalmings
sold and housed in this, the empire's

first museum. Alongside a nine-striped
armadillo, pangolin, two-headed goat,
a display of Peter's much-loved
beautiful butterflies now floats children's
severed heads in jars, a ghoulish
collection of defects and deformities
in glass cabinets. It is the artistry

of the still lifes that draws us in,
a cover story for our flagrant staring.
Ruysch's *liquor balsamicus* so refined
he was accused of sorcery, but behind
claims of Spirits of Zeus and Poseidon,
the secret to his liquor lies in clotted
pig's blood and mercury oxide.

Working closely with his midwives,
Ruysch gathered his specimens,
hoarding fetuses with extra limbs,
conjoined twins, infants with heads
enlarged and those sunken, a trove
of children's skeletons. The doctor
could not resist adding several

artistic flourishes: flowers and fishes,
bonnets and lace cuffs his daughter
assisted in placing on the delicate
skin. Freakish? Nay – ingenious!
Who else would (tastefully) place
a child's leg in the selfsame jar
as scorpion? Ruysch did. Impossible

as it is to choose among favourites,
one diorama eclipses the rest: a fetus
of about five months with placenta
in an antique jar decorated with coral,
a seahorse, an array of shells. You may
find it beside a woman's prepared
pelvic organs, her bladder and uterus.

MAYING

How are you beating in my body, heart?
How is it you dwell here? Guinevere
drew the colour from my skin like marble
carved from Porta della Pescheria's archivolt.
As lances bore toward her in the tower,
she ran from her abductors. Fair Winlogee,
catching my breath from these rattling lungs,
I never rode a horse to escape you; I only
clung to men to flee. Clutching these reins
so tightly they chafed me, Gwenhwyfar,
I too went a-Maying. Too rode from wood
to meadow, slipped a ring from my finger,
and fell into a sleep. It's no Arthur I need
now, no King of Tangled Wood, Malduc,
Melvis, or Lancelot to keep. Only pluck me
from these dreams before they burn me,
Findabair. I'll become Ellen Terry as Lady
Macbeth, a dress of beetle wings, crocheted.

FOUR OF CUPS

My arm bruised where the nurse drew
four vials of blood. It was a prick

to see if I pour out normally,
or if my mutant genes coagulate.

Patterns blur: my knuckles
against carpet at 1 AM, the next morning

waiting for the train carrying massive green tubes
to inch forward, then reverse, move forward again.

In this way, segments of the Keystone XL Pipeline
clear the intersection. Peering through

the fetal assessment unit's second storey window,
I watch a pigeon regurgitating crop milk

into her fledgling's gape. One bill fits within
the other, a keratin speculum.

Inside the examination room,
the specialist's tear-dropped window screen

resembles interconnected ovaries.
We cover up so pedestrians can't see

our naked bodies on the bed's off-white
wrinkled sheet. I dress and leave

and it finds us again outside the casino –
the train's waiting tunnel, endless and green.

DOVECOTE

Feet folded beneath my body
like the talons of a dove.
I don't speak its name and forget
the shape of its vowels on my lips.

Each step a hesitation,
the ice forming underneath.
My mother plucked out her hair.
The mourning dove, its feathers.

Calluses torn from my heels,
strips of skin pulled away.
The stillness of its body startled me,
the pigeon fallen to concrete.

Will you deny those who cannot speak
the mouthing of syllables?
It is the body's impulse to heal
before the mind perceives.

In the morning, each step stinging,
I walk toward uncertainty.
Collagen eschews a woven formation
for the scar's glassy alignment.

In the bathtub, my feet white
with bands of swollen tissue.
Forgetting is a kiss inverted,
a breath drawn from the lips.

Let me turn another corner
in this tender blue skin.
A drop of blood from its beak,
claws curled beneath its body.

A wound that never heals
but is torn open again and again.
That's what love is. Outside
my window, the endless cooing.

LAST WALK

Tired of wandering the same prairie
roads outside the city, tired of parking
on the same patch of flattened grass
beside the trail marker. Tired of climbing
over the barbed wire, tired of waiting
for trucks to pass before crossing the dirt
highway. Tired of brushing ticks off
the fabric of tucked socks, plucking not-yet
swollen abdomens. Tired of descending
into the branches. Tired of finding a way.
Tired of feeling limbs snap back as I follow
you toward a path, tired of reading the map.
Tired of squishing purple berries between
index finger and thumb, tired of feeling
numb. Tired of swatting flies, tired of saying
I'm thirsty, asking for a drink of water
from the bottle you carry. Tired of deciding
how much farther to go. Tired of taking
the same tired photo, tired of rusted tractors
parked in a more or less straight line,
tired of being tied to the grid superimposed
on the terrain, tired of crouching beside
a hole in the ground waiting for a glimpse
of something alive before turning away.

PRAYER FOR THE UNDOING OF SPELLS

With this ring, prompting mall jeweller
to deem me waitress in want of a talisman –

this ring invoking the superstition a vein
runs directly from fourth finger to heart –

this ring I had resized three times,
unable to adjust to the grip it held on me –

this ring I dream I wear again,
wriggling it back and forth over my skin –

this ring a nervous tic –
this ring reached for as I once reached for him –

this ring causing welt, inflammation, bruising –
this ring discovered stashed in a blue organza bag

and held in my palm, lighter than expected –
this ring a symbol, a stone, now shed

I DREAMED HE CAME OVER

With a two-year-old little girl
that was his and turned out to be yours too
and we didn't even know you had a baby
He was going to raise her
and you weren't going to be involved

IMMACULATE CONCEPTION

The Christ Child appeared to us true
to life, his wooden body finely carved,
then sanded, his skin painted and glazed,
blond hair falling in loose ringlets.
His fat cheeks blushed red as the apple
held in his hand, a slight cleft in his chin
inviting us to take him in. The cloister's
nuns commissioned for him cribs of gold
and silver, dressed the child in garments
of lace, silk, and satin, said their prayers,
then rocked him. Sister Margaretha
was gifted her doll upon taking her vows,
and woke to the child playing in his crib,
bidding that she hold him. She took him
in her arms, the poor thing. Did Mary
fare any better at pinning a cloth diaper
on the baby Christ's powdered bottom?
As the child cooed, she swaddled him.
He kissed and cuddled her, then said
solemnly: *If you do not nurse me,*
I will take myself away from you the moment
you love me the most! Margaretha held
the Christ Child against her bare breast
and he suckled cupid's bow on her nipple,
drinking. On Sunday, she organized
a pageant for the other lamb's brides:
the child resting in his crib of velvet finery
glimpsed a later-in-life version of himself
riding the palmesel into Jerusalem. Mounted
on an ass, his naked toes dangled above

the donkey's hooves, wheels of his cart
squeaking as his toy encircled the lavish crib.
Margaretha didn't anticipate the strangeness
of this encounter for the baby; the child
began fussing at the sight of his twin,
contorting at the palm fronds thrown.
As Margaretha burped him, his brow
furrowed at Older Jesus's majestic pose,
then his lips curled into a neat smile.
Was it happy recognition of divinity?
Gratitude for Margaretha who'd surely
grind her bones for his warming fire?
His passing gas sounded a squeal of relief.

ANNIVERSARY

In a Toledo cellar, two euros revealed ex-voto
of the Hand of Fatima with birds of paradise.

The last El Greco my husband showed me
was *Burial* as I sat in a pew, unmoved,

escaping the Eye of Conscience. We descended
on escalators cutting through ancient walls,

passed a pigeon's emaciated body,
Bosch-like and grotesque, its feathers bristled

from its needle beak. Beneath this gold ring
is a depression. Yours, a promise to throw it

in the sea, and moments later to always keep it,
the band I unearthed at the top of a mountain

as a preteen. On our third anniversary,
I changed my flight. We fought and cried.

Our trains went in opposite directions,
Bloomsday severing the thread it had tied.

Halfway from Toledo to Portugal,
I became a ghost in the empty seat
next to you. In Spain, my chest
tightened with clumped hair
and matted sheets, a round stone
wedged to my heel telling me
I had to leave. In my mind, I was
still crossing Lethe superimposed
on the Bow River where I once
watched you scatter a canister
of ashes and bone, and later crossed
its frigid water to escape a bear.
I feared the knee-deep current
would pull me away, not because
my interpretative skills are weak,
but because I believe my body
matches how I feel inside – flimsy.
I still think I can go back and find
you reading the *Tao* in the Madrid
laundromat, telling me I can't just
run away from the parts of myself
I like the least. But where outside
of oblivion will I ever find peace?
In any of those lonely train rides
through picturesque landscapes,
passing vineyards and churches
I saw only through your screen,
tell me, did you too feel free?

CATALOGUE

I was beside you at Mount Parnassus,
beside you at the Villa of Masks.
Beside you at the Bow River,
scattering your aunt's ashes.
I was beside you at Keats's apartment,
beside you at Maison Muzot.
Beside you in the streets of Paris,
the Appian Way, the catacombs.

I was beside you at Auschwitz-Birkenau,
beside you in the room of hair.
Beside you viewing the markings
the prisoners carved in the stone.
I was beside you in the hallway of faces,
beside you at the killing wall.
Beside you in a swarm of teenagers
riding the bus, singing Sean Paul.

GORGON

If the body slows when oxygen thins,
my skin solidifies to my particles' hardening.
Dying conquers in degrees; calcium ions

binding with protein ossify when adhered
to muscle, so skin turns to stone. The gorgon's
steady gaze anticipates rigor mortis. In breath's

choking, atoms tire, or as in decomposition
seep outside the body and are released. Death
is a transformation, my atoms indistinguishable

a table, this book, or tree. The ego
is freed in the sense that I breathe the same air
as Homer, the same fire Heraclitean –

but there is no me. Even the cells of my brain,
which holds the self, my personality,
are swapped out in seven-year cycles.

All that I seem to be could be shaken
by blood clot or incision, disrupted by an OD.
These are some of the things that hydrogen atoms do,

given fifteen billion years of cosmic evolution. Our bodies
in their movements cling to the concrete world,
a glimmer caught in a gorgon's petrifying stare.

SATURN RETURN

Before carving reindeer, walrus tusks,
before horses painted on cave walls,

all most early humans did was fashion
axe heads from hunks of chalcedony,

jasper, and flint, cryptocrystalline quarried
and hauled to the carving site. We worked

obsessively, breaking blocks of basalt
into hammerstones in teardrop shapes,

beating rock against rock, lithic flakes
falling like snow, layering skin with ash.

Was it ritual, pragmatic, a nervous tic?
One of us strayed from the carving site.

Another pulled a clamshell in two,
and found an iridescent whorl not unlike

the wash of green when we gazed
at the night sky. I wanted to hold him

like a brother, this artist, when I saw
him sleeping in the loam, but flattened

to the bog he appeared so lonely.
Were we all this alone? It was the sky

that called us forward, to depart
our planet's terrarium to celestial spheres.

The stars that lent us these atoms
would take our flicker of energy within.

We'd be calmed in our coming home,
like holding a slab of rock perfectly fitted

to our hands' flesh and striking stone.

LEAVING THE GARDEN

The museum bottlenecks
with bodies in the entranceway,

drones bumbling into one another.
This leg cramp that woke me up,

demon Rumpelstiltskin, pulls me apart
when you speak my name.

The lights dim as I stand before
The Garden of Earthly Delights, bigger

in person than on my leggings.
You linger in the antechamber,

gazing on *The Last Judgment* triptych:
two of its panels devoted to hell.

If the room is closing in it's because
it's too small for the both of us now.

The grey-brown ink of Bosch's warped
figures drew this study of monsters:

a thrown brochure setting our ship
of fools in flames as I thrash through

the fire for a lifeboat to cling to.
Bosch's grotesques – his beehive

and witches – were drolleries
in the margins of our melded book

of hours. We left the garden
and our life turned into grisaille panels

slamming shut. The creation
of the world sealed in a glass orb.

Earth and all its wonders closed.

THE UNICORN TAPESTRIES

As hunters enter the woods,
we wander the room of tapestries.
Medici's horn in the corner

casts a gleam that seizes our vision,
a narwhal tusk masquerading
as the unicorn's tapering wand.

The tapestries spin enchantment.
They snatch us toward *the start
of the hunt*, to a hundred species

of plants and beasts. We notice
daffodil and periwinkle, see
witches' broom, lady's mantle.

Meld, madder, and woad's
pigments of red, blue, yellow,
an artist's bed of dyes. The tapestry

depicts origins of its own making.
The lymerer collects scant droppings
as a scout signals from behind

a walnut tree to the extant hunting
party. *The unicorn is found.* We see
sage leaf and orange tree, antidotes

hinting that the unicorn purifies
the fountain's poisoned stream,
where a pair of pheasants now sip.

But the unicorn can't be disturbed
when conducting its magic.
The tree blossoms and bears fruit

in a single instance, a paradox
of fertility. Twelve hunters surround it
in conversation, their dogs in wait.

Goldfinches, a stag, and rabbits
lay before the flowing pillar spout
and cypher *AE*. We puzzle over

what the enigma means. Pot marigold
under the hyena's chin signals
disaster. Man watches animals

gather around the fountain. Ten
hunters approach the beast. *The
unicorn leaps out of the stream.*

An oak tree stands at centre scene.
AE glowers from four corners,
initials marking rumoured benefactors,

the aristocracy. A castle looms
in the background. A partridge
cheeps of thievery, the hunters'

spears brandished and thrust
at the unicorn's torso, enclosing
it. The beast is surrounded

by men, dogs, and greenery,
forcing *the unicorn at bay.*
It defends itself well. Horn

dipped, it gores a hound as it
kicks a hunter. Has the fruit
of the ripe orchards turned sour?

The heron, known for lofty
flight, is undisturbed by such
melee and poses serenely.

A single blood drop trickles
from a slit in the unicorn's coat
as spears strike from all sides.

We've heard only the purest
virgin can subdue a unicorn.
Otherwise, it remains invincible.

"Hail queen of the heavens."
If the unicorn represents Christ,
the hunter, Gabriel, then the maiden

motions to Virgin Mary. We see
the mystic capture of the unicorn
in two fragments. The handmaiden

distracts from the sole cameo
the virgin makes on the scene:
a glimpse of sleeve, her slender

fingers linger on the creature's
mane, the three enclosed within
the garden as menagerie. Behind

the gate, the scout blows a horn
from below an apple bough. The spell
is broken, the unicorn captured.

The unicorn bestows one last glance
to the absent maiden that fans
its coat, missing from the frame.

Stabbed by lances, echoing
Christ's passion, *the unicorn*
is killed and brought to the castle.

The scout catches blood drops
in his drinking gourd. A party
of men and women parade

the unicorn to the fortress,
its corpse slung over a horse's
saddle, one hunter fingering

its spiralled horn. The unicorn
is depicted both in the moment
of the sword blade's deathblow

and in the procession carrying
its corpse. Its trophy bears
a crown of thorns. In an instance

we see *the unicorn in captivity*,
the beast fenced in – wounds
replaced with pomegranate

seeds, blood with juice –
captive but seemingly content.
A woven chain around

its neck secures the unicorn
to a wooden pen, seated therein
amid white irises and Madonna

lilies, carnations and clove,
orchids and bistorts, dragonflies
dashing over the wallflowers

and white thistle, the cipher's
tasselled cord hanging from a tree,
bearing its riddle mysteriously.

LINE COMPOSED IN A DREAM

I thought there would be flowers

SUMMER PALACE

I eat buckwheat on the steps
of Peter's palace. Peasants' food,

a woman in the marshrutka consumes
raspberries on a tiny carving fork one by one.

I nap on a rounded topiary. She pierces
an apricot with a paring knife.

I'm a sucker for lavish fountains,
and shitting in opulent palaces.

Workers clean the vomit off the parquet floor.
A boy passes by with a bleeding schnozzle.

A kid with an eyepatch ogles the aviary.
It is a tourist's mission to photograph

all 144 fountains interspersed with WC.
It is a sickness, this luxury.

I opted against riding the meteors,
hydrofoil skipping on water as workers

in camo pound mallets into turf.

SWAN DIVE

The stagehand rouses the cardboard
bevy on conveyor belt across the rear
of Swan Lake's ground row, gliding

through the scenery. A woman kneels
in secret from the KGB, prodding
her son away from the peephole

in Akhmatova's shared suite. Cue
White Nights and Tchaikovsky
on no sleep. We lower the periscope

of Morskoi Boi's arcade submarine
and pull the trigger, inflicting maximum
damage to enemy ships, all of which

are attached to moving chains. In praise
of war games and long-eroded links,
we ride Soviet-era elevators not yet

on last legs to catch the tram's
yearly decreasing fleet and descend
into the second subway's fallout shelter.

The company comes out for yet another
curtain call, the third circle disturbed
by ringing cellphones. Peel back the skin

to the proscenium's inner workings:
all of life's a teaser and tormentor,
a stage decorated in azure, gilt, crystal.

Only the elderly theatre attendant
flashing laser beams from balcony
to Tsar's box can thwart the tourists'

stolen frames. A Fabergé egg filled
with a ticking grenade. We pull out
the last stops, the pin still in place.

AUTOMATON

Of the silver swan dipping its beak
in a sea of waves to catch a metal fish,
much has been written: how the water
glinted, the creature's movement so realistic
one might mistake the swan for elaborate
disguise. Among the memorable automata
comes to mind the famous digesting duck
(lost to history), a bronze-gilt elephant,
cuckoos eternalized in YouTube clips.
But mechanisms fully functioning or not,
nothing tops the golden Peacock Clock
ensconced in a glass aviary. In its forest
menagerie, a dragonfly perches on fungi,
as squirrel feeds on acorn and impish fox
rests on oak branch. To witness a technician
climb inside the cage and wind the device,
rousing the peacock to life, is pure delight.
The peafowl cranes its slender neck, turns
to fan its feathers, and dazzles audiences
with the splendour of its train. Flanked by
owl and cockerel, the trio greets morning's
arrival, beaks singing to ringing chimes.

RUSSIAN ARK

I facetime Nathan from the Italian
Cabinet. He has Wi-Fi in his pocket,
walking the forested mall in Kyoto
to the movies. We turned divorce
into a contest to see who can run
farthest away, only to reconcile
via pixels of frozen screens. I call
him from St. Isaac's Colonnade,
a boat on a canal on the Fontanka,
comforted by the bridges stitching
together the islands of this city.
I eschew all guided tours, my map
sticky from my water bottle spilling
on the pack of Orbit in my bag.
Equipped with just 30 gigs of Wi-Fi,
I make a beeline to catch glimpses
of masters' canvases and malachite.
Not far from *Crouching Youth*,
I intuit ghosts in the Romanovs'
Hall of Portraits, do a double take
at the bronze bust of a Roman's
missing eyes, linger in the Raphael
Loggias' kaleidoscope of grotesques.
Black-and-white photographs strewn
throughout the Hermitage depict
blank frames of a city under siege.
There's the Bolsheviks storming
the rococo dining room, Catherine
dashing from theatre to toilet,
the Golden Age sequestered away.

We end our call in the rotunda
after I share the Rembrandts
through my iPhone's shaky lens.
Sit with the Rubens a little longer
for me. I walk backwards down
the stairwell, and into the sea.

THE OBSERVER EFFECT

Relegate to the dreams of one day
the life you thought you would lead.

This, the thought before sleep:
there will be no children.

Was it because you stand too close to paintings
you developed this piecemeal thinking?

He found you on the back steps
leaning against the door and brought you in,

peeled the plastic from your eyes.
This too was love.

When is it brave to turn away
and when is it foolhardy?

It wasn't enough to acknowledge
you are capable of cruelty

– you had to enact it.
You could have gone a lifetime

without knowing that side of yourself.
You chose to stare your shadow in the face,

and this too was bravery.
Is there any part of language that sustains?

Every word's an elegy.
He gave permission to set down

the burden of the past.
The act of seeing was one of change.

BLANKET CREEK

The corpse flowers are late this year.
Slow to uncurl their waxy stems,
heads lobbing under the weight of sleep,
underground in their winter graves.

Now that I hear the trees speaking
it's with reverence I return.
Lay me down on the cedar's fur,
magnified on skin, little water bear.

The tree's burl is its bullocks,
threads of moss its pubic hair.
The ferns sway as they fornicate.
The tardigrades survive the war.

I missed the embryonic ghosts.
I let you go ahead of me.
I deemed your passage swift.
There were flickers of happiness.

I have worn my father's clothing.
I have willed our oaths reversed.
It's a narrow tree-lined path,
and at the end of it, a burst.

NOTES

Drolleries is another term for grotesques, or small drawings of human-animal hybrids that appear in the marginalia of illuminated medieval manuscripts.

"Aspect of Saturn" borrows an English translation of a Latin anagram used by Christiaan Huygens to disclose his discovery of Saturn's rings.

"Leaving the Atocha Station" takes its title from the Ben Lerner book.

"I Dreamed He Came Over" quotes my mother.

"Gorgon" quotes Carl Sagan.

"Russian Ark" takes its title from the Alexander Sokurov movie of the same name.

ACKNOWLEDGEMENTS

Thanks to Kevin Connolly for your incisive edits, guidance, and faith in my poems.

Thank you to Kelly Joseph, Dionne Brand, and everyone at M&S.

Thank you to Nathan Mader for your support, friendship, and conversation, and providing essential edits, insight, and advice on the book. Thank you to Credence McFadzean, Jake Byrne, and Karen Solie for your helpful edits on many of these poems. Thanks, as well, to Mark Levine and Andy Axel for your assistance in shaping an earlier version of the book.

Thank you to the Saskatchewan Arts Board and the Access Copyright Foundation for providing financial assistance. I am grateful for a Canada Council Travel Grant to attend The Banff Centre, and for the publishers who approved funding through the Ontario Arts Council Recommender Grants program. Thanks to the Saint Petersburg Art Residency (SPAR) for providing the space to write some of these poems.

Thank you to the editors of the journals who published earlier versions of some of these poems: *BAD NUDES*, *Big Smoke*, *BOAAT*, *Canadian Literature*, *Canthius*, *carte blanche*, *CV2*, *Diode*, *Event*, *The Fiddlehead*, *Green Mountains Review*, *The Humber Literary Review*, *Juniper*, *Numéro Cinq*, *Prelude*, *PRISM international*, *Room*, *This Magazine*, *untethered*, *The Walrus*, and *Witch Craft Magazine*.

Thanks to the editors of *Best Canadian Poetry in English 2016* for including "Nymph."

Thank you to my parents and brothers, and my friends in Toronto and Regina.